T0055082

THE PRICE OF PEACE

Stories From Africa

Many of the characters in these stories from Africa are looking for something, perhaps a peaceful marriage, or just a new pair of shoes. But everything comes at a price. In Sierra Leone, Ajayi and his mistress Ayo have lived peacefully together for many years. Why change things? A bus conductor in Malawi sees no escape from the boredom of an endless journey, while two sisters in Ghana, living in troubled times, disagree about the way to live their lives. Then there are two families of exiles living in Zimbabwe. They dream of returning to their homeland, but reality can be very different from the dream. And last, in the crowded capital of Nigeria, an extraordinary thing happens on Makinde's lot, and before long Makinde wishes he could return to his old peaceful life . . .

BOOKWORMS WORLD STORIES

English has become an international language, and is used on every continent, in many varieties, for all kinds of purposes. *Bookworms World Stories* are the latest addition to the Oxford Bookworms Library. Their aim is to bring the best of the world's stories to the English language learner, and to celebrate the use of English for storytelling all around the world.

Jennifer Bassett
Series Editor

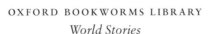

OXFORD BOOKWORMS LIBRARY
World Stories

The Price of Peace

Stories from Africa

Stage 4 (1400 headwords)

Series Editor: Jennifer Bassett
Founder Editor: Tricia Hedge
Activities Editors: Jennifer Bassett and Christine Lindop

NOTES ON THE ILLUSTRATORS

MESHACK ASARE (illustrations on pages 5, 12, 27, 32, 38, 59, 66, 71) was born in 1945 in Ghana. He studied Art, and later Social Anthropology, and was a teacher for many years. He is now a very well-known writer and illustrator of children's books, and travels widely through Africa looking for different African cultures to represent in his stories. His books have won numerous awards, including Noma and UNESCO awards, and have been published in many countries.

JOSEPH NTENSIBE (illustrations on pages 19, 45, 51) was born in 1951 in Uganda, East Africa. A freelance artist for many years, he works in oils, ink, pencil and charcoal, and watercolours, and his artworks have been shown in galleries in Kenya and the USA.

RETOLD BY CHRISTINE LINDOP

The Price of Peace

Stories from Africa

OXFORD UNIVERSITY PRESS

OXFORD
UNIVERSITY PRESS

Great Clarendon Street, Oxford OX2 6DP

Oxford University Press is a department of the University of Oxford.
It furthers the University's objective of excellence in research, scholarship,
and education by publishing worldwide in

Oxford   New York

Auckland   Cape Town   Dar es Salaam   Hong Kong   Karachi
Kuala Lumpur   Madrid   Melbourne   Mexico City   Nairobi
New Delhi   Shanghai   Taipei   Toronto

With offices in

Argentina   Austria   Brazil   Chile   Czech Republic   France   Greece
Guatemala   Hungary   Italy   Japan   Poland   Portugal   Singapore
South Korea   Switzerland   Thailand   Turkey   Ukraine   Vietnam

OXFORD and OXFORD ENGLISH are registered trade marks of
Oxford University Press in the UK and in certain other countries

ISBN: 978 0 19 479198 4

A complete recording of this Bookworms edition of
The Price of Peace: Stories from Africa is available

Printed in China

ACKNOWLEDGEMENTS

The publishers are grateful to the following for permission to adapt and simplify copyright texts:
Dr Olu Nicol and the Estate of Abioseh Nicol c/o David Higham Associates Limited for
'The Truly Married Woman' by Abioseh Nicol from *Modern African Stories*,
ed. Charles R. Larson (Collins/Fontana Books 1978); the author for
'The Road to Migowi' from *Malawian Writers Series No. 6 Waiting for a Turn*
(Popular Publications, Malawi 1981); the author for 'Two Sisters' from *No Sweetness
Here* by Ama Ata Aidoo; the author for 'Blood Feuds' by Paul Tiyambe Zeleza from
The Joys of Exile (Stoddard Publishing, Toronto); the author for 'The Miracle Worker' by
Sefi Atta (www.eclectica.org/v7n4)

Illustrations by: Meshack Asare (pp 5, 12, 27, 32, 38, 59, 66, 71)
and Joseph Ntensibe (pp 19, 45, 51)

*We have made every effort to trace and contact all copyright holders before publication,
but if notified of any errors or omissions, the publisher will be happy to rectify these
at the earliest opportunity.*

Word count (main text): 16,068 words

For more information on the Oxford Bookworms Library,
visit www.oup.com/elt/gradedreaders

CONTENTS

NOTE ON THE LANGUAGE

There are many varieties of English spoken in the world, and the characters in these stories from Africa sometimes use non-standard forms or sentence patterns. This is how the authors of the original stories represented the spoken language that their characters would actually use in real life.

There are also a few words that come from African languages (for example, *kachasu* from Chichewa). These words are either explained in the stories or in the glossary on page 73.

THE TRULY MARRIED WOMAN

ABIOSEH NICOL

A story from Sierra Leone, retold by Christine Lindop

*People who live together get used to each other.
They have daily routines, and the usual patterns of
life go on without much change.*

*Ajayi and Ayo have been together for twelve
years. They are not married; Ajayi had meant to
marry Ayo but somehow the right moment never
came. He is quite comfortable with things as they
are; maybe a little too comfortable …*

Ajayi sat up and looked at the cheap alarm clock on the chair by his bedside. It was six fifteen, and light outside already; the African town was slowly waking to life. The night watchmen, hurriedly shaking themselves out of sleep, were busily banging the locks of shops and houses, to prove to their employers that they were at work. Village women were walking through the streets to the market place, arguing and gossiping.

Ajayi tasted his cup of morning tea. It was as he liked it, weak and sugary, without milk. He got up and walked to the window, and took six deep breaths. Doing this daily, he believed, would prevent diseases of the chest. Then he took a quick bath, taking water from a bucket with a metal cup.

By then Ayo had laid out his breakfast. Ayo was his wife. Not really a wife, he would explain to close friends, but a mistress. A good one. She had given him three children and was now pregnant with another. They had been together for twelve years. She was a patient, handsome woman, very dark with very white teeth and open honest eyes. Her hair was always neat and tidy. When she first came to him – against her parents' wishes – he had truly meant to marry her as soon as she had had their first child, but he had never quite found time to do it. In the first year or so she would tell him in detail about the marriages of her friends, looking at him with hopeful eyes, but he would attack her friends' wild spending and the huge cost of the ceremony, and soon she stopped.

Ajayi and Ayo went to church regularly, and two or three times a year the priest would speak out violently against unmarried couples living together. Then their friends would feel sorry for them, and the men would say that the church should keep out of people's private lives. Ajayi would stay away from church for a few weeks, but would go back after a while because he liked the singing and he knew secretly that the priest was right.

Ayo was a good mistress. Her father had hoped she would marry a high-school teacher at least, but instead she had chosen a government clerk. But Ayo loved Ajayi, and was happy in her own slow, private way. She cooked his meals and bore him children. In what free time she had she did a little buying and selling, or visited friends, or gossiped with Omo, the woman next door.

With his towel round his waist, Ajayi marched back to the bedroom, dried himself and dressed quickly in his pink silk suit. He got down the new bottle of medicine which one of his friends had suggested to him. Ajayi believed that to keep healthy, a man must regularly take medicine. On the bottle were listed about twenty very different diseases and illnesses. All of these conditions would disappear if the patient took this medicine daily. Ajayi believed that he had, or was about to have, at least six of these diseases. It also said on the bottle that a teaspoonful of the medicine should be taken three times a day. But Ajayi only remembered to take it in the morning, so he took a big drink from the bottle. The medicine had a bitter taste, and Ajayi was pleased – that obviously meant that it was good strong medicine.

He went in to breakfast. When he had finished, he beat his eldest son, a ten-year-old boy, for wetting his sleeping-mat in the night. Ayo came in after the boy had run screaming out of the door.

'Ajayi, you beat Oju too much,' she said.

'He should stop wetting the sleeping-mat, he is a big boy,' he replied. 'Anyway, no one is going to tell me how to bring up my son.'

'He is mine too,' Ayo said. She did not often disagree with him unless she felt strongly about something. 'He has not stopped wetting although you beat him every time he does. In fact, he is doing it more and more now. Perhaps if you stopped beating him, he would get better.'

'Did I beat him to begin doing it?' Ajayi asked.

'No.'

'Well, if I stop beating him, how will that stop him doing it?' Ajayi said, pleased with his own cleverness.

'You may have your own opinion,' Ayo said, 'but our own countrywoman Bimbola, who has studied nursing in England and America, told us in a women's group meeting that it was wrong to punish children for such things.'

'All right, I'll see,' he said, reaching for his sun hat.

All that day at the office he thought about this. So Ayo had been attending women's meetings. *That* was a surprise. Always looking so quiet, and then telling him about the modern ideas of overseas doctors. He smiled. Yes, Ayo was certainly a woman to be proud of. Perhaps it was wrong to beat the boy. He decided not to do so again.

Towards closing time the chief clerk sent for him. Wondering what trouble he was in, he hurried along to the office. There were three white men sitting on chairs by the chief clerk, who was an older African man dressed very correctly. Ajayi's heart started to beat loudly. The police, he thought; oh God, what have I done?

'Mr Ajayi, these gentlemen have asked for you,' the chief clerk said.

'Pleased to meet you, Mr Ajayi,' the tallest said, with a smile. 'We belong to the World Gospel Crusading Alliance from Minnesota in the USA. My name is Jonathan Olsen.' Ajayi shook hands and the other two men were introduced.

'You expressed an interest in our work a year ago and we have not forgotten. We are on our way to India and we thought we would come and see you personally.'

The boat on which the men were travelling had stopped

'*Bimbola told us in a women's group meeting,*' said Ayo,
'*that it was wrong to punish children for such things.*'

for a few hours near Ajayi's town. The chief clerk looked at Ajayi with new respect. Ajayi tried desperately to remember any contact with WGCA (as Olsen now called it) while he made polite conversation with them. Then suddenly he remembered. Some time ago a friend who worked at the United States Information Service had given him a magazine which contained an invitation to join the WGCA. He had written to the WGCA asking for information, but really hoping that they would send free Bibles which he could give away or sell. He hoped at least for large religious pictures which he could put up on his bedroom wall. But nothing had happened and he had forgotten about it. Now here was WGCA in person. Three persons. At once he invited all three and the chief clerk to come to his house for a cold drink. They all agreed.

Olsen suggested a taxi, but Ajayi quickly told him that the roads were too bad. He had already whispered to another clerk to hurry home on a bicycle and warn Ayo. 'Tell her I'm coming in half an hour with white men, and she should clean up and get fruit drinks.'

Ayo was confused by this message, as she believed all white men drank only whisky and iced beer. But the messenger said the visitors were friendly, religious-looking men, and he suspected that perhaps they were missionaries. Also, they were walking instead of being in a car.

That explained everything to Ayo, and she started work at once. Oju was sent with a basket on his head to buy fruit drinks. Quickly she took down the calendars with pictures of lightly clothed women, and put up the family photographs instead. She removed the magazines and put out religious books, and hid the wine glasses under the sofa. She just had time to change to her Sunday dress and borrow a wedding ring from her neighbour when Ajayi and the visitors arrived.

The chief clerk was rather surprised at the change in the room – which he had visited before – and in Ayo's dress and ring. But he hid his feelings. Ayo was introduced and made a little conversation in English. This pleased Ajayi greatly. The children too had been changed into Sunday suits, faces washed and hair brushed. Olsen was delighted and took photographs for the WGCA magazine. Ayo served drinks and then left the room, leaving the men to discuss serious matters. Olsen began to talk enthusiastically about Ajayi's future as a missionary.

The visit went well and soon the missionaries left to catch their boat. Ajayi had been saved from a life as a missionary by the chief clerk, who explained that it was against the rules for government workers. Ajayi could even be sent to prison, he said. The missionaries were saddened but not surprised by this news.

The next day Ajayi took the chief clerk a carefully wrapped bottle of beer as a present for his help with the visitors. They discussed happily the friendliness and interest the white men had shown.

This visit, and Ayo's protest about the beating, made Ajayi very thoughtful for a week. He decided to marry Ayo. Another reason was the photo that Olsen had taken for his magazine. In some strange way Ajayi felt he and Ayo should marry, as millions of Americans would see their picture as 'one god-loving and happy African family'. He told Ayo about his marriage intentions one evening after a particularly good meal. Ayo at once became worried about him. Was he ill? she asked. Was there anything wrong at the office? No, he answered, there was nothing wrong with wanting to get married, was there? Or was she thinking of marrying somebody else? Ayo laughed. 'As you like,' she said; 'let us get married, but do not say I made you do it.'

They discussed the wedding that night. Ajayi wanted Ayo to have a traditional white wedding dress, with a veil, and flowers, but Ayo decided, sadly, that it was not right for a mother of three to wear white at her wedding. They agreed on grey. Ayo particularly wanted a corset because she did not want to look too huge; Ajayi gave in on this. But there would be no holiday after the wedding; he said they could not afford it, and one bed was as good as another. Ayo gave in on that. But they agreed on a church wedding.

That evening Ajayi, excited by the idea and the talk about the wedding, pulled Ayo to him as they lay in bed.

'No,' said Ayo shyly, pushing him back gently, 'you mustn't. Wait until after the marriage.'

'Why?' said Ajayi, rather surprised, but obedient.

'Because it will not be right,' Ayo replied seriously.

When Ayo's father heard of the coming marriage, he made Ayo move herself and everything she owned back to his house. The children were sent to Ayo's married sister. Most of Ajayi's family welcomed the idea, except his sister, who was worried that Ayo would become more important in the family than she was. She advised Ajayi to ask a soothsayer to look into the future. As Ayo heard about this from friends in the market, she saw the soothsayer first and fixed things. When Ajayi and his sister called at night to see him, the soothsayer looked into Ajayi's future and saw a happy marriage, but avoided the sister's eye. She smiled bitterly and accepted defeat.

The only other problem was Ayo's neighbour Omo, who had always lent Ayo her wedding ring when Ayo needed one in a hurry. She had suddenly turned cold, particularly when Ayo showed her the wedding presents Ajayi was going to give her. Omo's face was both jealous and angry as she touched the silky, see-through material.

'Do you mean you are going to wear these?' she asked.

'Yes,' Ayo replied simply.

'But, my sister,' she protested, 'suppose you had an accident and all those doctors lifted your clothes in hospital. They will see everything through these.'

'I never have accidents,' Ayo answered, and added, 'Ajayi says all the Hollywood cinema women wear these.'

'These are awful; they hide nothing, you should be ashamed to wear them,' the jealous girl said, pushing them angrily back over the wall to Ayo.

'Why should I want to hide anything from my husband when we are married?' Ayo said, winning the argument and moving happily back to her own kitchen.

The arrangements had to be made quickly, since time and the tightness of the corset were both against them. Ajayi missed his normal life, particularly his morning cup of tea. He borrowed a lot of money to pay for the music, the food, and the dresses that Ayo and her sisters would wear on the wedding day.

The day before the wedding, Ajayi's uncle and other relations took a Bible and a ring to Ayo's father. They took with them two small girls carrying on their heads large gourds, which contained things like pins, small coins, fruit, and nuts. These were traditional gifts to the bride from the bridegroom, so that in future arguments Ayo could not say, 'This terrible man has given me neither a pin nor a coin since we got married.'

On arrival at Ayo's father's house, the small group passed it first, pretending to be uncertain, then returned to it. Ajayi's uncle then knocked several times. Voices from inside asked for his name, the name of his family, and his reason for coming. He told them. Half an hour of discussion and argument followed. Was Ajayi's family good enough? Ajayi himself was waiting at home, but his relations enjoyed the argument and pretended to be frightened. At last Ayo's father opened the door. It should now be clear to Ajayi's relations that this was a family that was proud, difficult, and above the ordinary.

'Why have you come here?' asked Ayo's father.

Ajayi's uncle answered:

> *We have come to pick a red, red rose*
> *That in your beautiful garden grows,*
> *Which never has been picked before,*
> *So lovelier than any other.*

'Will you be able to take good care of our lovely rose?' asked another relation.

Ajayi's family replied:

> *Such good care shall we take of your rose*
> *That many others will grow from it.*

They were finally allowed into the house; drinks were served, the gifts were accepted, and others given. For thirty minutes they talked about everything except the wedding. All through this, Ayo and her sisters and some other young women were kept hidden in a bedroom. Finally Ayo's father asked what brought Ajayi's family to his house.

'We have heard of a beautiful, obedient woman known as Ayo,' said Ajayi's uncle. 'We ask for her as a wife for Ajayi.'

Ayo's father opened the bedroom door and brought out Ayo's sister.

'Is this the one?' he asked.

Ajayi's relations looked at her carefully.

'No, this one is too short to be Ayo.'

Then a cousin was brought out.

'Is this the right woman?'

'No, this one is too fat.'

About ten women were brought out, but none was the right one.

'It was a good thing we asked to see her,' said Ajayi's uncle, turning to his relations, 'or we could get the wrong woman.' The relations agreed.

'All right,' said Ayo's father. 'Don't be impatient; I wanted to be sure that you knew who you wanted.' With tears in his eyes he called Ayo out from the bedroom, kissed her, and showed her to Ajayi's family.

'Is this the girl you want?' he asked.

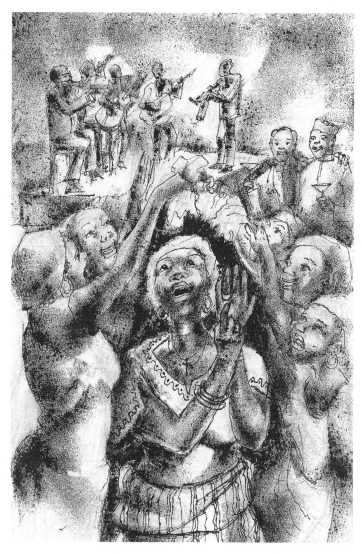

As she stood in the centre of the circle, in a ceremony that
she had stopped dreaming of for herself, Ayo cried with joy.

'This is the very one,' Ajayi's uncle replied with joy.

'Hip, hip, hooray,' everyone shouted, dancing in a circle round Ayo as the music started. And as she stood in the centre, a woman in her mid-thirties with slightly grey hair, in a ceremony that she had often seen but had stopped dreaming of for herself, Ayo cried with joy, and her unborn child moved inside her for the first time.

The next morning the women of her family helped her to wash and dress. Her father gave her away at the marriage ceremony in church, a quiet wedding with about sixty people present. Afterwards they went to Ayo's family home for the wedding meal. At the door one of Ayo's old aunts met them and gave them a glass of water to drink from – first Ajayi, then Ayo.

'Do not be too friendly with other women,' she told Ayo, 'because they will steal your husband. Live peaceably together, and do not let the sun go down on an argument between you. And you, Ajayi, remember that a wife can be just as exciting as a mistress! And do not use violence against our daughter, who is now your wife.'

By now everyone had arrived, and they went into the house for the European part of the ceremony. The wedding cake (which Ayo had made) was cut, and then Ajayi left for his own family home. Later he returned for Ayo. The women cried as they said goodbye to her.

'When it comes to the true work of a woman – having children – nobody can say that you are not enthusiastic,' said Ayo's mother through her tears.

Ajayi and Ayo visited various relations on both sides of

the family and at last they were home. Ayo seemed different in Ajayi's eyes. He had never really looked at her carefully before. Now he saw her proud head, her long neck, her handsome shoulders, and he held her to him lovingly.

The next morning, as his alarm clock went off, he reached for his morning cup of tea. It was not there. He sat up quickly and looked. Nothing. He listened for Ayo's footsteps outside in the kitchen. Nothing. He turned to look beside him. Ayo was there. She must be ill, he thought; all that excitement yesterday.

'Ayo, Ayo,' he cried, 'are you ill?'

She turned round slowly, still lying down, and looked at him. She moved her feet under the cotton bedcover, getting comfortable. There was a terrible calm about her.

'No, Ajayi,' she replied, 'are you? Is something wrong with your legs?'

'No,' he said. He was alarmed, thinking that all the excitement had made her go a little crazy.

'Ajayi, my husband,' she said, 'for twelve years I have got up every morning at five to make tea for you and breakfast. Now I am a truly married woman, you must behave towards me with a little more respect. You are now a husband and not a lover. Get up and make yourself a cup of tea.'

THE ROAD TO MIGOWI

KEN LIPENGA

A story from Malawi, retold by Christine Lindop

Boring jobs are the same the world over. Doing exactly the same thing day after day after day can destroy you.

The man who tells this story works as a bus conductor on a route between towns in Malawi. He has been doing this job for nine years, but it feels like a hundred years . . .

At Chitakale the bus, although already packed full, picks up a few more passengers and continues on its way. The road is wet and the March rain beats gently but endlessly upon the roof of the bus. Outside, the yellow maize stands in the fields, unmoving, drunk with too much rain. The rainy season, dark, long and heavy, is coming to an end, and soon people will be coming to cut the maize.

But neither the muddy road nor the maize in the field can show me anything new or interesting. For nine years I have been a bus conductor, and I cannot begin to count how many times during those nine years I have been on this road. Whether it is the rainy season as now, or a dry September afternoon, or a cold June morning, it is all the same to me.

I always have one wish, and it never changes: to get to the end of the journey as quickly as possible. And yet I never get my wish. I know the life history of every bridge, every stone, and every tree on the road from Limbe to Migowi, I promise you. My past is on the road, so is my present, and I find it hard to imagine a future away from this road, the road to Migowi and back to Limbe, and back again to Migowi . . .

I don't enjoy thinking about my past before I became a conductor. I know I once had a father and a mother. We once lived on one of the large tea estates in Mulanje. But in my mind this time is distant, not clear. My father died when I was a little boy, and my mother lived on, selling *kachasu*, illegal beer, to pay for my schooling. When she had finished doing that, she drank herself to death on the day I went home with my first pay.

I also had an elder brother who went to work in the mines in South Africa. At first we used to write, then my brother stopped answering my letters, so I stopped writing.

The bus stops, and I loudly ask if there is anyone getting out here. There is no answer, so the driver starts his engine and the bus moves on. But a moment later someone rings the bell and again the bus stops.

'I'm dropping here,' says a man rising up from a seat not far away from me.

Several passengers shout rude, angry words after the man as he pushes his way to the exit. I say nothing to him and as a result some of the ugly words are thrown at me too.

Before I became a conductor, I worked in a tea research station. My job was to sit all day and write down the figures produced by a strange and complicated machine which, I was told, measured the brownness of tea. I never understood what those figures meant, or how the machine worked, but my boss repeatedly told me that my job was of great importance to tea research. I did not understand this either, though I was proud to play my part in this great work. However, I quickly grew tired of sitting in the same place and writing down the same figures day after day, and I left the job after only a year. 'I want an interesting job,' I told my friends as I left. 'I'm going to be a conductor; there is variety there, different people, different places every day.'

The bell once again rings and the bus stops for some passengers to get off.

'I have a bicycle on the roof,' says one man.

'And I have a bag of maize,' says another.

I'm sure I know the reason why I am growing so thin: my ears have grown tired of hearing such things. I have heard them hundreds, no, thousands of times. Maybe one day the passengers will be kind enough not to say them.

The bus has reached the worst part of the road and is moving at walking speed. The driver swings it from one side of the road to the other as he tries to keep to the less muddy parts. Many a time the wheels go deep into the mud, and all the passengers have to help in pushing the bus out.

'I wonder what time we'll get to Migowi,' I say aloud without meaning to.

The driver, hearing me, looks at his watch, ashamed. 'By five o'clock we should be there,' he says.

The driver is a very old man, has been a driver for over thirty years, and should not still be working, although all attempts by the National Transport Company to make him stop have failed. No one understands why this strange old man, who is said to be very rich, prefers to go on working. I suspect he will die as soon as he is taken off the road. Behind the wheel he looks full of life, but his eyes show the shadow of death; it is only the road that keeps him alive.

The bus slides in the mud on a steep hill and nearly turns over. Streams of water run down the side of the road.

'Everyone come out and push . . .'

It seems to me that the road changes everybody, no one is free of it; not just the driver, but all the passengers I have ever met. I feel sorry for them, but the thought worries me.

I became a conductor in order to escape from a boring job, and a cold impersonal machine that measured the brownness of tea. But after nine years I do not find much variety in the brownness of men. Indeed, it seems to me that these are the same passengers that I left Limbe with on that rainy morning nine years ago.

That rude talkative man has been on the same back seat for nine years, and is still telling the story of his business success. So too that other man near the window, who smokes all the time but won't let the windows be opened. That crying child never seems to grow up. And there is that fat woman, who cleverly pushes off everyone attempting to sit next to her . . . Yes, these are the same passengers, and it is the same road, the same journey without end.

'Everyone come out and push.'

The rain continues to fall and the driver keeps swinging the bus from one side of the road to another, to avoid the mud. The bus complains continuously under the heavy load

Many a time the wheels go deep into the mud.
'Everyone come out and push.'

of passengers, which never seems to get less. People get on and get off, but the bus is always crowded.

At Kambenje the bus stops to pick up a few passengers, wet with rain. Among them is a man wearing an old yellow raincoat. I look at him carefully as he gets on. Yes indeed! My father! My father had just that hardened look on his face, that bent back from years of picking tea. And for the first time in these nine years, I see before me a clear picture of my father, my mother, my brother, our little house on the estate, the fruit trees in front of the house, the red roof of the factory in the distance, and the black smoke coming out of it, everything to the last detail.

I hear the singing of the workers as they pick tea leaves in the fields, in their rough yellow raincoats, with baskets on their backs. I feel now as I felt then: respect for these workers who, with their songs, make hard work and hard lives seem so pleasant. A feeling of joy suddenly fills me. I move over to where the man is standing and touch his shoulder.

'Father!' I shout, and I feel the tears coming out of my eyes. I turn and smile at everyone in the bus, and I see my joy shining back from their faces. Oh, what a beautiful world! The sound of the rain on the roof and the complaining engine have become sounds of joy, the old man at the wheel has become happiness itself. The voices of the passengers and the crying of the child fill me with a wonderful feeling.

'Father!'

So my father and mother have never died after all, my

brother has never had to go to South Africa, and I myself have never had to write down figures from a machine that measures the brownness of tea . . .

But suddenly the bus comes to a violent stop, and all the standing passengers fall over one another. I try to stay on my feet by holding on to the man I had called my father, but he is already falling and he pulls me down with him. Everything in my dream disappears; I seem to be coming back from the dead as I and the man I had called my father help each other to our feet.

'Everyone get out and push.'

The bus has once again got trapped in the mud; the two front wheels are in so deep that it is going to take hours before we can continue.

'By seven o'clock we should be at Migowi,' says the driver, when we have finally succeeded in pulling the bus out.

Once those words used to calm me down. But now as I hear them I feel cold all over. The idea of arrival has now begun to frighten me. I say nothing, and instead look at the maize in the fields outside.

TWO SISTERS

AMA ATA AIDOO

A story from Ghana, retold by Christine Lindop

Life is not much fun if you work as a typist in an office, and you earn so little that you can't even buy yourself a nice pair of shoes. A girl needs shoes. A girl needs a boyfriend with a nice fast car, and a nice fat wallet.

So Mercy finds a boyfriend who suits her needs. The trouble is, her big sister – sensible, married Connie – won't like it at all …

As Mercy puts the cover on her typewriter, the thought of the bus ride home goes through her like a pain. It is her luck, she thinks. Everything is just her luck. If she had one of those university boys for a boyfriend, wouldn't he come and take her home every evening? Certainly, Joe would love to do exactly that – with his taxi. And he is as handsome as anything, and a good man, but you know … A taxi is a taxi. The possibility of the *other* man actually coming to fetch her – oh well. She knows it will take some time before she'll be brave enough to ask for things like that from *him*. But it's hard not to think about it. Would it really be so dangerous? Doesn't one government car look like another – the hugeness of it, the dark glass, the driver in uniform? She can already see herself stepping out of the car to greet the other girls, who look at her with eyes like knives. To begin with, she will be a little more careful. The driver can drop her under the *neem* trees in the morning and pick her up from there in the evening . . . anyway, she will have to wait a little while for that and it is just her bad luck.

So for the meantime it is going to be the local bus with its dirty seats, unpleasant passengers, and rude conductors . . . Jesus! She doesn't wish herself dead or anything as stupidly final as that. Oh no. She just wishes she could sleep deep and only wake up on the day of her first car ride to work.

The new pair of black shoes are more sensible than their owner, though. As she walks out of the office, they sing:

Count, count, count your blessings.
Count, Mercy, count your blessings
Count, Mercy, count your blessings
Count, count, count your blessings.

They sing out of the office, along the road, and into the bus. And they start singing again along the path as she opens the front gate and walks to the door.

'Sissie!' Mercy called.

'*Hei* Mercy.' And the door opened to show the face of Connie, her big sister, six years older, and now heavy with her second child. Mercy dropped into the nearest chair.

'Welcome home. How was the office today?'

'Sister, don't ask. Look at my hands. My fingers are dead with typing. Oh God, I don't know what to do.'

'Why, what is wrong?' asked Connie.

'You tell me what is right. Why should I be a typist?'

'What else would you be?'

'What a strange question. Is typing the only job there is in this world? You are a teacher, are you not?' said Mercy.

'But . . . but . . .'

'But what? It's my fault – is that what you're saying? I didn't do well enough in the exams, so I can't be a teacher. Or even a secretary.'

'Mercy, what is the matter?' said Connie. 'What have I done? Why have you come home so angry?'

Mercy broke into tears.

'Oh, I'm sorry, Sissie. It's just that I am sick of everything. The office, living with you and your husband. I want a husband of my own, children. I want . . . I want . . .'

'But you are young and beautiful. And marriage – well, it's you who are delaying it. Look at all these people who are running after you,' said Connie.

'Sissie, I don't like what you are doing. So stop it.'

'Okay, okay, okay.'

And there was a silence.

'Which of them could I marry?' said Mercy. 'Joe is – mm, fine – but, but I just don't like him.'

'Little sister, you and I can be truthful with one another. I am not that old or wise, but I can advise you a little. Joe drives someone else's car now. Well, you never know. Lots of taxi drivers own their taxis in the end, sometimes more than one.'

'Of course. But what a pity that you are married already. Or I could make a date for you – with Joe!'

And they both burst out laughing. It was when Mercy got up to go to the bedroom that Connie noticed the new shoes.

'*Ei*, those are beautiful shoes. Are they new?'

From the other room, Mercy's voice came and went as she undressed and then dressed again. But that was not the reason for the uncertainty in her voice.

'Oh, I forgot to tell you about them. In fact, I was going to show them to you. I think it was on Tuesday I bought them. Or was it Wednesday? When I came home from the office, you and James had taken Akosua out. And later I forgot all about them.'

'I see. But they are very pretty. Were they expensive?'

'No, not really.' Mercy's answer came too quickly.

And she said only last week that she didn't have a penny on her, thought Connie. And I believed her because I know what they pay her is just not enough to live on. I've been thinking she manages very well. But these shoes . . . And she is not the type who would borrow money just to buy a pair of shoes; she would just wear her old pairs till things got better. Oh, I wish I knew what to do. I mean, I'm not her mother. And I wonder how James will see these problems.

'Sissie, you look worried,' said Mercy.

'Hmm, when don't I? With the baby coming in a couple of months and the government's new controls on pay. On top of everything, I have dependable information that James is running after a new girl.'

Mercy laughed. 'Oh, Sissie. You always get dependable information on these things. But men are like that.'

'They are selfish.'

'No, it's just that women allow them to behave the way they do instead of taking some freedom themselves.'

'Well if I had the chance to behave the same way,' said Connie, 'I wouldn't make use of it.'

'But why not?'

'Because I love James. I love James and I am not interested in any other man.' Her voice was full of tears.

But Mercy was amused. 'Oh God. Now listen to that. It's women like you who keep all of us down.'

'Well, I'm sorry but it's how the good God made me.'

'Mm. I'm sure I can love several men at the same time.'

'Mercy!'

They burst out laughing again. And yet they are sad. But laughter is always best.

Mercy complained that she was hungry and so they went to the kitchen to heat up some food and eat. The two sisters alone. It is no use waiting for James.

'Sissie, I am going to see a film.' This from Mercy.

'Where?'

'The Globe.'

'Are you going with Joe?'

'No.'

'Are you going alone?'

'No.'

Careful, Connie.

'Who are you going with?'

Careful, Connie, please. Your little sister's eyes are looking angry. Look at the sudden lines around her mouth. Connie, a sister is a good thing. Even a younger sister. Particularly when you have no mother or father.

'Mercy, who are you going out with?'

Careful, Connie. Your little sister's eyes are looking angry.
Look at the sudden lines around her mouth.

'Well, I had food in my mouth. And I had to finish it before I could answer you, no?'

'I am sorry.' Connie's voice is soft.

'And anyway, do I have to tell you everything?'

'Oh no. It's just that I didn't think it was a question I was not allowed to ask.'

There was more silence. Connie cleared her throat and waited, afraid.

'I am going out with Mensar-Arthur,' Mercy said.

As Connie asked the next question, she wondered if the words were leaving her lips. 'Mensar-Arthur?'

'Yes.'

'Which one?'

'*How many do you know?*'

Something jumped in Connie's chest and she wondered what it was. Perhaps it was the baby.

'Do you mean that politician?' she said.

'Yes.'

'But, Mercy . . .'

Little sister only sits and chews her food.

'But, Mercy . . .'

Chew, chew, chew.

'But, Mercy . . .'

'What?' said Mercy.

'He is so old.'

Chew, chew, chew.

'Perhaps, I mean, perhaps that really doesn't matter, does it? But they say he has so many wives and girlfriends.'

Please, little sister. Your private life is not my business, but you just said yourself that you wanted a man of your own. That man belongs to so many women already . . .

That silence again. Then there was only Mercy's footsteps as she went to wash her plate, and then left the kitchen. Tears ran down Connie's face. She heard Mercy having a bath, then getting ready to leave the house. The shoes. Then she was gone. Connie hadn't meant to start an argument. What use is a sister, if you can't have a talk with her? And what would their parents say if they were alive? They were good church-goers. They feared God. Running around with an old and evil politician would horrify them.

A big car arrived outside the house, a huge machine from the white man's land. The sound of its super-smooth engine was soft and gentle, unlike the hard banging of the girl's high-heeled shoes. When Mensar-Arthur saw Mercy, he reached across and opened the door to the passenger seat. She sat down and the door closed with a smooth little sound as the car slid away.

After they had gone a mile or so from the house, the man started a conversation.

'And how is my darling today?'

'I am well.' But everything about her said bad news.

'You look serious today, why?'

She remained silent and still.

'My dear, what is the matter?'

'Nothing.'

'Oh.' He cleared his throat. 'Eh, and how were the shoes?'

'Very nice. In fact, I am wearing them now. They feel a little small, but then all new shoes are like that.'

'And the handbag?' he asked.

'I like it very much, too ... My sister noticed them. I mean the shoes.' Now the bad news was out.

'Did she ask you where you got them from?'

'No.'

He cleared his throat again. 'Where did we agree to go tonight?'

'The Globe, but I don't want to see a film.'

'Is that so? Mm, I am glad because people always notice things.'

'But they won't be too surprised.'

'What are you saying, my dear?'

'Nothing.'

'Okay, so what shall we do? Shall I drive to the Seaway?'

'Oh yes.'

He drove to the Seaway, to a part of the beach they knew very well. She loves it here, with the wide sandy beach and the old sea. She has often wished to drive very near to the end of the sands until the tyres of the car touched the water. A very foolish idea, as he said sharply to her the first time she mentioned it. It was in his 'I-am-old-enough-to-be-your- father' voice. There are always disadvantages. Things could be different. If she had a younger lover ... Handsome, maybe not rich like this man here, but with enough money to afford a fast car. A car like the ones she has seen in films, with tyres that can do everything ... and they would drive to exactly where the sea and the sand meet.

'We are here,' he said.

'Don't let's get out. Let's just sit inside and talk.'

'Okay. But what is it, my darling?'

'I have told my sister about you,' said Mercy.

'Good God. Why?'

'I couldn't keep it to myself any longer.'

'Childish. It was not necessary at all. She is not your mother,' he said.

'No. But she is all I have. And she has been very good to me.'

'Well, it's her duty. A sister's duty.'

'Then it's *my* duty, a sister's duty, to tell her about something like this. I may get into trouble.'

'Don't be silly,' he said. 'I normally take good care of my girlfriends.'

'I see,' she said, and for the first time in the one month since she agreed to be this man's lover, the tears which suddenly rose into her eyes came there naturally.

'And you promised you wouldn't tell her.' It was Father's voice now.

'Don't be angry. After all, she was sure to hear it one day.'

'My darling, you are too wise. What did she say?'

'She wasn't happy.'

'Don't worry. Find out something she wants very much but cannot get in this country.'

'I know for sure she wants an electric motor for her sewing machine.'

'Mm. I am going to London next week on government business, so if you bring me the details of the machine, I shall get her the motor.'

'Thank you.'

*The old Sea moves further up the sands, but the rising water
cannot reach the tyres of the car.*

'Oh, and let me know as soon as you want to leave your sister's place. I have got you one of the government houses.'

'Oh . . . oh,' she said, pleased for the first time since this awful day had begun.

Down on the beach, the old Sea slides up and down the sands. He takes no notice of humans. He has seen things happen along these beaches. Different things. The same things. He never does anything about them. Why should he? People are unimportant. Here is a fifty-year-old 'big man' who thinks he is somebody. And a twenty-three-year-old child who chooses a silly way to fight life's problems. As they play with each other's bodies on the back seat of the car, the old Sea shuts his eyes, bored. He moves further up the sands, but the car is parked safely away from the sea, and the rising water cannot reach its tyres.

James has come home late. But then he has been coming back late for the past few weeks. Connie is crying and he knows it as soon as he enters the bedroom. He hates tears, because, like many men, he knows they are one of the strongest weapons that women have.

'James.'

'Oh, are you still awake?' He quickly sits beside her. 'Connie, what's the matter? You've been crying again.'

'James, where were you?'

'Connie, I have warned you about this. I won't let you question me like a prisoner every time I am a little late.'

She sat up. 'A little late! It is nearly two o'clock.'

'Anyway, you won't believe me if I tell you the truth.'

She lies down again and turns her face to the wall, and James throws himself down beside her.

'James, there is something much more serious.'

'You have heard about my newest affair?'

'Yes, but that is not what I am talking about.'

'Jesus, is it possible that there is anything more important than that?'

And as they laugh, they know that something has happened. One of those things which, with luck, will keep them together for some time to come.

'But James, what shall I do?'

'About what?'

'Mercy. She is having an affair with Mensar-Arthur.'

'Wonderful.'

'James, we must do something about it. It's very serious.'

'Why shouldn't she?'

'But it is wrong. And she is ruining herself.'

'Since every other girl she knows has ruined herself and made money out of it, why shouldn't she? Her friends don't earn any more than she does, but every day they wear new dresses, shoes, and so on, to work. What do you expect her to do?'

'The fact that other girls do it doesn't mean that Mercy should do it too.'

'You're being very silly. If I were Mercy, I am sure that's exactly what I would do. And you know I mean it, too.'

James is cruel. Terrible. Mean. Connie breaks into fresh tears, and James puts his arm around her. There is one thing he must make her understand, though.

'In fact, tell her to stay with him. He may be able to speak to someone in your government office so that after the baby is born you can keep your job there.'

'James, you want me to use my sister!'

'She is using herself, remember.'

'James, you are terrible.'

'And maybe he would even agree to get us a new car from abroad. I shall pay for everything, but that would be better than that old car I was thinking about. Think of that.'

'You will ride in it alone.'

'Well . . .'

That was a few months before the coup. Mensar-Arthur did go to London and bought something for all his wives and girlfriends. He even remembered the motor for Connie's machine. When Mercy took it to her, she was quite confused. She had wanted this thing for a long time, and yet one side of her said that accepting it was wrong. She could not discuss the whole business with Mercy, and James always took Mercy's side. She took the motor with thanks; the price she paid was her silence about Mercy. In a short while, Mercy left the house to go and live in the government house that Mensar-Arthur had managed to get for her.

Then, a couple of weeks later, the coup. Mercy left her new place before anybody could throw her out. James never got his car. Connie's new baby was born. Of the three, Connie was happiest with these changes. In her eyes, Mensar-Arthur and everything that went with him meant trouble for her sister and for her own feelings too. Now things could return to normal. Mercy would move back to the house, perhaps find a man who was more – ordinary, let's say. Then she would get married and these terrible times would be forgotten. God is good, he brought the coup before her sister's affair became widely known and ruined her name . . .

The arrival of the new baby has ended all the difficulties between James and Connie. He is that kind of man, and she that kind of woman. Mercy has not been seen for many days. Connie is beginning to get worried . . .

James heard the baby's loud cries the moment he opened the front gate. He ran in, holding the few things he had bought on his way home.

'We are in here,' called Connie.

'I certainly could hear you. If there is anything people in this country have, it is a big mouth.'

'Don't I agree? But we're well. He's eating normally and everything. You?'

'Nothing new. More stories about the ex-politicians.'

'What do you mean, nothing new?' said Connie. 'Look at the excellent job the soldiers have done, cleaning up the country of all that dirt. I feel free already and I can't wait to get out and enjoy it.'

James laughed bitterly. 'All I know is that Mensar-Arthur is in prison. No use. And I'm not getting my car.'

'I never took you seriously on that car business.'

'Honestly, Connie, don't you want me, your husband, to be successful and get rich?

'Not out of my sister's ruin.'

'Ruin, ruin, ruin! Christ! See, Connie, the funny thing is

that I am sure you are the only person who thought it was a disaster to have a sister who was the girlfriend of a big man.'

'Okay; now all is over, and don't let's argue about it.'

'Was it you who arranged the coup, I wonder? Just because of your sister? It wouldn't surprise me.'

And Connie wondered why he said that with so much bitterness. She wondered if . . .

'Has Mercy been here?' asked James.

'Not yet, later, maybe. Mm. I had hoped she would move back here and start all over again.'

'I am not surprised she hasn't. In fact, if I were her, I wouldn't come back here either. Not to listen to endless good advice from big sister, no thank you.'

'Mercy is my only sister. I can't sit and see her life going wrong without feeling it. I'm grateful that something put a stop to that. What worries me now is that she won't tell me where she's living. She talks about a girlfriend but I'm not sure that I know her.'

'If I were you, I would stop worrying because it seems Mercy can take care of herself quite well,' said James.

Then there was the sound of a car stopping outside the house. Ah, but the footsteps were unmistakably Mercy's. Are those shoes the old pair which were new a couple of months ago? Or are they the newest pair? And here she is herself, the pretty one. A happy, smiling Mercy.

'Hello, hello, my people!' And she goes straight to the baby. 'Dow-dah-dee-day! How's my dear young man today? Grow up fast and come to take care of Auntie Mercy.'

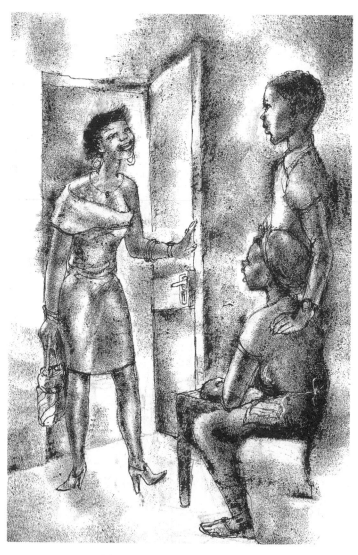

And here she is herself, the pretty one.
A happy, smiling Mercy.

Both Connie and James cannot take their eyes off her. Connie says, 'He says to Auntie Mercy he is fine.'

Still they watch her, horrified, and wondering what it's all about. Because they both know it is about something.

'Listen, people, I brought a friend to meet you. A man.'

'Where is he?' from James.

'Bring him in,' from Connie.

'You know, Sissie, you are a new mother. I thought I'd come and ask you if it's all right.'

'Of course,' say James and Connie, and for some reason they are both afraid of what is coming.

'He is Captain Ashley.'

'Which one?'

'How many do you know?'

James still thinks it is impossible. 'Eh ... do you mean the army officer who has just been given the job of ... of ...'

'Yes.'

'Wasn't there a picture in *The Crystal* over the weekend of his daughter's wedding? And another one of him with his wife and children and grandchildren?' said James.

'Yes,' said Mercy.

Connie just sits there with her mouth open that wide ...

BLOOD FEUDS

PAUL TIYAMBE ZELEZA

A story from Zimbabwe, retold by Christine Lindop

No one who has not felt it can understand the pain of an exile. Living in a country that is not your own, among people who are not your people. Always a foreigner, an outsider, someone who does not belong.

Two families, living in Zimbabwe, but the country they call home is Malawi, a country they have not seen for nearly thirty years, a sad, troubled country ...

*O*f course my father and Uncle Phala had their little disagreements. But they were the usual ones among friends. Then there were all those moments of loneliness, of no hope at all, that everyone in exile feels. But they always survived, because they missed home so much. They never doubted they would return one day.

That was all my father and Uncle Phala dreamed about: the return to their own country. They talked about home all the time. How they grew up. The games they used to play. The schools they went to. The fight for freedom.

'You young ones have no idea what we had to do to get rid of the British,' Uncle Phala used to tell us whenever he could. He was proud of the injury to his leg, which he said he got in a street battle against the government in the 1950s. And then my father, of course, felt he had to show us the marks on his back, which he got from beatings in prison.

'I was in prison for a week,' he would say proudly, 'not like others who only got injured in a fight.' Over the years his time in prison became a month, six weeks, then a year.

'Don't listen to him,' Uncle Phala would answer. 'He fell out of a tree. That's how he got those marks!' And he would break into a great, deep laugh.

'Now I'll tell you how he *really* got his injury!' my father would say, also laughing. And they would go on like this.

It wasn't just that they liked each other – it was much more than that. They called each other brother. It was twelve years or more before I learned that Uncle Phala was, in fact, not my real uncle. He and my father had met in the mining village in Zimbabwe where I was born and grew up.

Their two families lived together in a flat as big as a matchbox, and my brothers and sisters and I grew up and went to school with Uncle Phala's children. When we finished school, I and most of my brothers became miners and lived in the mining village.

All through their years in Zimbabwe my father and Uncle Phala were involved in exile politics. It began with the mining village's Home Burial Society. This helped workers from our home country in times of trouble, particularly burials. Years later my father and Uncle Phala joined the National Redemption Movement. This was an organization of exiles who were against the government back home.

When I was a young boy, I sometimes went with my father

and Uncle Phala to the beer hall where the Movement held its meetings. They were both good organizers and fine speakers. Whenever one of them rose to speak, the hall became silent and people listened to every word. After they finished speaking, everybody would clap, and I felt so proud of them. When they stopped working as miners at the age of fifty, they began working full-time for the Movement, which grew quickly, thanks to a large exile community.

Over the years the news from home got worse. We heard of arrests, violence, and worse. It was not the government that my father and Uncle Phala had fought for when the British left in the 1960s and our country finally became independent.

'In the beginning,' my father remembered, 'we loved them. We loved the government. We thought it was ours.'

I remember Uncle Phala telling us when we were small about the day of independence.

'Everything seemed so beautiful that day. The sunshine felt a little gentler, the skies were bluer, the plants were greener, and the air smelled fresher. Just before midnight the British flag was taken down, and our flag was raised as thousands clapped. We loved every word our leader spoke. We called him "the saviour" – we thought he would save us.'

Like so many other people, my father and Uncle Phala spent all the money they had to go to the capital for the independence ceremony – a great day for our country.

At that time my father worked on a farm. Soon afterwards he lost his job when the farm was sold to one of the new government officers who preferred to employ workers from his own part of the country. Uncle Phala lost his job because he was the leader of a workers' organization at his factory. The new government did not allow workers' organizations any more, saying that the workers had no enemies now that independence had been won.

So Uncle Phala and my father left the country a couple of years later, as so many others had done before them, to look for jobs in the mines of Zimbabwe.

The exiles in Zimbabwe learned to live with the bad news that came from home. They would discuss it and pass it on, but it was something they did not actually experience. Although exile was painful, they could hide behind it and dream, and avoid being responsible for their own lives.

I did not think of myself as one of them. Of course, I considered where my parents came from as my homeland too, although I had never been there. But I also felt strong ties to Zimbabwe, the place of my birth. At home we spoke my parents' language; elsewhere we used one of the local languages.

I never really had to think much about my *real home* until I was an adult. It didn't matter when I was a child. Of course, the other children would sometimes call us by rude names – whatever word was fashionable for 'foreigners' at the time – but it never mattered to me. Not so in later years. It was partly age, I suppose. As you grow older, things seem to hurt a little deeper.

The situation in Zimbabwe was also changing. People began to think of themselves less as *Africans* and more as

Zimbabweans. We became 'foreigners', even those of us who were born in Zimbabwe, when it came to giving out jobs and to finding someone to blame for the nation's problems.

That is when I became more involved in the National Redemption Movement. Slowly, our community turned inward, and as far as possible we kept together, helped one another, and married among ourselves.

I married Uncle Phala's eldest daughter, Mwali, which pleased both our parents greatly. 'We are now real brothers!' the two men told everyone at the wedding ceremony.

I began to miss my homeland as much as my father and Uncle Phala did. I wanted to know more about it. So I asked questions; I searched for information in books, newspapers, and magazines. I dreamed of the shining lake with its golden sand beaches, the rivers, hills, and mountains, and the cool green highlands. A land, as my father and Uncle Phala remembered it, of tidy villages, handsome cities, safe streets, and smiling faces. Not this dry, empty land that was only good for exiles.

We hoped and dreamed. In the meantime I grew older. I had three children. My father and Uncle Phala began to look like the grandfathers they were. They continued to be involved in the Movement, but the situation in our homeland stayed the same. None of us thought it would change soon, although we did not doubt that change would come in the end. Nobody imagined how quickly the thirty-year-old regime would fall a few years later.

People had been unhappy for years, of course, but it was the church leaders who brought it into the open. One Easter

*It was the church leaders who brought it into the open, reading out
a letter in churches throughout the country.*

Sunday the priests read out a letter in churches throughout the country. The letter did not ask for anything unusual, just simple things like respect for the law, freedom for political prisoners, food for the hungry . . . But the letter hit the country like a bomb. No one had ever demanded these things openly before. Some church leaders were arrested and terrible warnings were given.

But it was too late. The students, young and impatient, joined the fight. 'Give us free elections!' they demanded. 'Let political prisoners go free!' The universities and colleges were closed and the students were sent home. That only made things worse, because the students took the message back to their home towns.

Then the workers joined the battle. They stopped work, demanding better pay. The police tried to break up one protest march, but they only succeeded in shooting hundreds of workers and starting angry protests all over the country. Even foreign governments and banks began to talk about sending no more money to a regime that had lost control.

I had never seen my father and Uncle Phala so excited. They had the radio and television on all the time, following the news from home. For some reason I was not as excited as I had expected. I had become so used to hoping and dreaming that the possibility of return frightened me. Exile had always been my life. It was all I knew.

Other things made me uneasy too. Our community of exiles began to break into two groups: those who wanted to return, and those who were not so enthusiastic. The same disagreements were seen in families, and before long in the

Movement itself. At our yearly meeting there were so many arguments that by the end the Movement had broken into three separate groups. It was sad to watch.

Nothing prepared me for what was waiting for us in our dear homeland. It was certainly beautiful, but that was all. We went first to my father's village. I was disappointed. It was nothing more than a group of rough mud houses. I met some of my uncles and aunts for the first time. They all looked much older than my father, although they were younger than he was. They were nice and friendly, but that was all they could offer us. It was the same at my mother's village, which was a few miles away.

I felt like a stranger. Our relations called us *machona*, meaning the long lost people. As *machona*, we were expected to bring endless presents, far more than the workers who returned every two years or so, carrying huge suitcases full of gifts for their relations – clothes, blankets, radios, watches, sunglasses . . . For a couple of months they would live like chiefs. Then, when all their money had gone, they would leave for Zimbabwe once again. But we disappointed our relations. I suspected that this was one of the reasons that my father had not returned for so long.

I also began to understand that my own people were no different from the people of Zimbabwe, who had many arguments and fights between their different ethnic groups. We were proud that our community of exiles in the mining village had no silly ethnic arguments of that kind, although we had people who came from different places and ethnic groups in the homeland. My father, for example, was from the south, and Uncle Phala from the north. But back in our own country I heard the same sad, silly arguments.

In fact, it was more serious than that. All our politicians, old and new, seemed to want to make trouble between the different ethnic groups. Perhaps this was because no political party had any real ideas or plans for our country's future.

My father, of course, soon got involved in politics. At first he was busy trying to start a business with the money he had brought back from Zimbabwe. Then someone asked him to be a leader of one of the local parties. He said no at first, but I think that was only because he did not want to seem too enthusiastic.

'Well, I have to do what is best for my people,' he said in the end. 'They need a man of my experience for leadership.' It was good for his business. Many of the local businesses here in the south were owned by northerners, and people were beginning to dislike this more and more.

A few weeks later I went north with my family to visit Uncle Phala. We were well received. Uncle Phala proudly introduced me to his relations. I liked his village better than my father's. The place and the people seemed less miserable. Mwali and I decided to make our home there and start a business. I bought two lorries to take fish from the lake to the capital. It would make me a lot of money.

My father was not pleased with my plan when I returned for a visit. He said I was turning my back on my people.

'But Father,' I protested, 'we're living with Uncle Phala. He's your "brother", remember?'

'Uncle Phala is all right. It's his people who aren't.'

'I can't believe you, of all people, saying that.'

I did not tell Uncle Phala about my father's opinions. He was pleased that we had decided to stay.

'You're my favourite son. You've been good to my daughter.' Uncle Phala did not have a son. All of his eight children were girls.

Like my father, he had also started a business, which was doing quite well. Before long he, too, was asked to join a leading local political party. And like his 'brother', he waited for a while before he agreed.

And so the two most important men in my life became caught in the new politics. Each party tried to organize bigger meetings, bigger marches than the others; no one discussed plans for government. Political prisoners, locked up in prison, were almost forgotten, except by their mothers. And no party called for national discussions on how to bring good government to our poor, weak, unhappy country.

It was difficult not to be part of the noisy business of politics, but I tried to stay out of it. I missed the quieter politics of exile. Here there was no hoping, no dreaming – it was all rough and real. Too rough, in fact.

A couple of months before the elections were held for a new government, violence broke out. It was not clear who started it. Northerners accused southerners, and southerners accused northerners. Both sides chased the 'foreigners', the outsiders, living among them. Church leaders and others blamed the government for making the troubles worse. The government, of course, said that they were not responsible.

Our "saviour", now a very sick old man, said the violence proved he was right. It showed that party politics and elections were as foreign to the country as winter.

One morning we were woken by a noise like a bomb exploding. We looked out of the window. My lorries were on fire. We all knew why, but we blamed thieves for it. It was less painful that way. We were trying to keep the hopes and dreams of exile alive, but we could not hide from the real world any longer. That evening Uncle Phala spoke what was on our minds.

'You're not safe here. Maybe you should go home.'

'I thought I was home,' I said, more in sadness than in anger.

'So did I. This isn't the country your father and I left thirty years ago. They've changed it into something else, something terrible, that will eat us alive if we aren't careful.' For the first time he looked very old.

'We'll be out of here as soon as we can.'

'No, you'll go alone. Mwali and the children will be as unsafe in your home as you are here.'

'But I can't leave my family behind.'

'It's for their own good, and for your own good too,' he said sadly. 'Believe me.'

'It's not right,' I said softly. 'It's just not right.'

He did not look at Mwali or me, but I could see that he agreed.

Mwali and I spent a sleepless night discussing the matter. We decided that we would either stay together or leave together. Nothing would separate us.

One morning we were woken by a noise like a bomb exploding.
My lorries were on fire.

But we did not have time to tell Uncle Phala what we had decided, because early the next morning we heard a large crowd shouting excitedly outside.

'We want the southerner!' they screamed. 'We want the southerner! Give us the southerner!'

'Hide under the bed quick,' Mwali whispered.

The shouting came closer, and some people started banging on the door. Then the noise stopped, and we heard Uncle Phala's voice. 'He ran away last night!'

'No!' the crowd shouted with disappointment. 'We want the southerner!'

'You know how these southerners are!' Uncle Phala shouted. 'They don't know what "brave" means. They may be good with books and take all the jobs for teachers and clerks, but that's all they can do. They can't fight. That boy may have balls, but he's no braver than a woman.'

The crowd laughed.

'Leave the house alone.' Suddenly he called out Mwali's name. 'Come and tell these brave sons of the north where your useless husband is.'

I could not believe what he was saying. Had he gone crazy?

'What should I do?' she asked me desperately.

'I don't know. What's wrong with your father? I thought he loved me. He told me so himself.'

'Mwali! Please come out and tell these men where your good-for-nothing husband went.'

I felt suddenly angry. 'Go. He's your father.' I pushed her and she started crying. 'Go, I said!'

'Don't scream. They'll hear you.' She tried to get herself under control. 'Please stay where you are. Don't move,' she said as she went unwillingly to the door.

'See, she's crying,' Uncle Phala said when she came out. 'I told her not to marry a southerner!' The crowd began to go away, still shouting about southerners. Moments later Mwali returned, looking both shaken and thankful.

I stayed indoors the whole day. Later Uncle Phala came to me. I could see the unhappiness on his face. 'I'm sorry I had to say all those things.'

'So you didn't mean it,' I said coldly.

'Of course not.' He was trying not to cry. 'That was the only way I could save you, by talking their kind of language. You'll always be my favourite son, no matter what.'

I do not know how long we sat there, staring at the walls. We all wished to be back in the old days of exile.

I escaped that night, and my people were thankful to see me safe.

'I always told you that northerners are cruel and wild,' my father said. I could not remember him ever saying that. But I did not feel like arguing with him. I just wanted to sleep and dream of the simpler days of exile.

The elections were held on time. The old governing party just managed to win, but the other political parties refused to accept the results and did not recognize the government. While this argument went on, the army appeared on the streets, and the frightened country became calm.

It seemed safe enough for me to ask Mwali and the children to come. Uncle Phala came with them.

When the two old men met, they put their arms round each other. For a while it seemed like the old days, except that they both looked so much older now. They were both much thinner. Uncle Phala walked even more painfully, and my father could not see or hear very well.

But it was not the old days. They had little to talk about. It was painful to watch. The friendliness and the laughter had all gone. The days of exile now seemed so far away and unreal. And yet we had been back for about a year.

Uncle Phala only stayed a couple of days. He left early in the morning. We all went with him to the bus station, except for my mother who was not feeling well. My father and Uncle Phala stood in silence with their arms round each other for what seemed like a long time. From the steps of the bus Uncle Phala waved to us with his stick. We waved in return. Then he climbed painfully onto the bus and never looked back.

THE MIRACLE WORKER

SEFI ATTA

A story from Nigeria, retold by Christine Lindop

Making a living on the streets of Lagos is not easy. There are so many people coming and going, chasing work, looking for God …

Bisi has found God; her husband Makinde hasn't, and isn't looking for him either. But the unexpected can always happen, whether you call it a miracle or not …

Makinde only complained about one thing in his new wife Bisi: she gave too much in tithes to her church. Ten per cent was not enough for Bisi. She had to prove just how religious she was, and each time she visited her church, the Abundant Life Tabernacle, she gave a little extra money for the married women's group, which in Makinde's eyes was just a home for gossips.

Makinde was a mechanic. He worked on a lot, a piece of ground on the corner of a Lagos street. Bisi sold bread and boiled eggs to passengers at a nearby bus station. When she stopped wearing colourful clothes and started dressing in black, Makinde didn't complain. When she stopped speaking to those of his friends who did not go to church, he didn't say anything. When he broke his hand, Bisi went without food to make his hand better. He had jumped out of the way of a motorcycle taxi and hit his hand on a rock. For two weeks Makinde ate his own food, and Bisi's food as well, and his finger got better, but it stayed bent.

Bisi could get too enthusiastic about religious things, Makinde thought. So that afternoon when she came to his lot with his usual lunch of bread and boiled egg, and she saw the windscreen of an old car that had been sitting there for years, and she fell on her knees, saying it was a vision of the Virgin Mary, Makinde didn't even look up from his sandwich. He had cleaned the windscreen with an oily rag to get rid of some bird's droppings, and later in the morning there had been some light rain.

Bisi ran to the bus station to tell passengers she'd seen a vision. Several of them came back to see. A few, mostly men, walked away laughing about Nigerian women and their love of religion. The rest, women mostly, stayed to stare at the dirty windscreen. They trembled and burst into tears. It was a miracle, they said. There was a clear figure all right: one small circle over a bigger circle, and beautiful rainbow colors around the small circle. More bus passengers arrived as news of the vision got out. Soon they were enough to make Makinde's work impossible, and he drove them away.

All his life he had worked, and he never went to school. First, he sold oranges, then at age ten he began working for his father, a mechanic. He put air into tyres and mended them, then he learned about engines. He was not the best mechanic in Lagos, but people knew that when they left their cars with him, things would not go missing.

Some of his customers seemed extraordinary to him.

They were rich from oil money, and owned Mercedes cars, but when it was time to pay Makinde, they counted every single coin. They gave him the money with soft fat fingers, while Makinde couldn't even remember the colour of his own fingernails. He had black oil under them. He ate Zero-One-Zero to save money: nothing for breakfast, one big lunch meal, nothing for dinner. Here was the real miracle. He was still poor.

'My wife,' he said to Bisi after the visitors left. 'I don't care if you choose to throw away your money on your church – actually I do, but nothing I say will change your mind. But I won't allow you to do your church business here, on my lot, and get in the way of my work.'

'Why?' Bisi asked.

'Your people will frighten my customers away with their crying and shaking.'

'How?' Bisi asked.

This was the way she argued: she asked enough questions to drive him crazy, hoping that she would win.

'All I'm saying is that it must never happen again,' Makinde answered.

He was known as a patient man, because he didn't like talking; talking was too tiring. Bisi knew he didn't change his mind easily either. He refused to go to church with her.

The next day Makinde arrived at work and a group of about twenty people were waiting in his lot, men, women, and children, all dressed in white.

'We have come to see the vision,' an old man said.

'In the name of God,' Makinde said to himself.

It was about five thirty in the morning. This news hasn't come to them from Bisi, thought Makinde; it's gone from one person to the next. He had not expected that.

'I'm sorry,' he said. 'You can't come and pray on my lot.'

'Unfortunately that is out of your control,' the old man said. 'Something stronger than you or me has chosen this place. It's probably best not to stand in its way.'

The old man was smiling, but Makinde was afraid anyway.

'Over there,' he said.

He pointed at the old car, once a Peugeot 405. Robbers had taken the seats and steering wheel. The group walked towards the windscreen. The old man saw the vision first and fell on his knees. The group followed, and then they began to sing. Makinde started beating a piece of metal to drown the sound. At most, he thought, five groups would visit his lot. Three that day, and maybe two the next.

He'd heard about such visions that appeared on dirty glass where poor people lived. He could not read, so he did not know what the newspapers in Lagos said about these visions. Reporters said that the visions drew great crowds, or Throngs, and that these throngs came together, or Flocked. These were past national headlines:

Throngs Flock to Vision of Mary on Toilet Window.

Throngs Flock to Vision of Mary on Food Shop Window.

Makinde's guess – five groups of twenty people – was too low. Two hundred and fifty people visited his lot in the morning. By afternoon about five hundred people had been to his lot. Makinde stopped showing them the windscreen of

*The group began to sing. Makinde started beating
a piece of metal to drown the sound.*

the Peugeot. A tall thin woman stayed from her morning visit to act as a guide. She told the story to a reporter: how Makinde and his wife were recently married, how Bisi was religious and Makinde did not go to church. This vision had still appeared on his lot, and this was a clear sign that God's love was everywhere, for everybody.

Bisi came at lunch time with Makinde's usual lunch of bread and egg. She saw the crowds and immediately said that she was not responsible. 'It wasn't me!'

'Don't worry, I believe you,' Makinde said. The situation was out of her control.

The guide woman approached her. 'God's blessings to you, my sister.'

'To you too,' Bisi said.

'We've been here all morning, without pay, showing the people where to pray for miracles.'

'Yes?'

'Yes, and we are getting quite hungry now, so please can you go back and get some bread and eggs for us to eat?'

The guide said 'we', but she was talking about herself alone. The miracle that *she* had prayed for was for people to stop saying she was crazy. She knew that her job was to do God's work. Anywhere else in the world she would be able to stand in the street and tell people about God. Here she was sent to a hospital, where the doctors laughed at her and the nurses beat her up.

Makinde told Bisi to get her bread and a boiled egg. Bisi left to fetch the food, and the woman returned to the crowd. Then an idea came to Makinde. Without pay, the guide had said. The people were standing on his lot, getting in the way of his work. Why not make them pay? They paid to go to church. He added up the numbers. If each visitor paid him one *naira*, he thought, that would more or less cover the money he was losing because he couldn't work.

He stood in front of his lot and said politely, 'Excuse me? I am Makinde. Yes, em, the owner of this lot. I have decided I will not get in the way of your praying today. But I . . . I am not a rich man, as you can see, and all these crowds are, em, causing problems for my business. Yes, what I'm suggesting is that . . . can you . . . can you please . . .?'

Talking was exhausting him. Nobody was listening anyway. They were praying, singing, shaking.

Makinde tried shouting. 'My name is Makinde! I'm the owner of this lot! And I'm telling you now! If you wish to continue to see your vision, I suggest you pay me one *naira* now, each, or else I will take a rag and clean the vision off.'

The lot went quiet. One or two people asked what he was talking about and why he was getting angry. The guide woman was explaining to them when another visitor arrived. Makinde put out his hand without looking at her face.

'It's one *naira* to enter, please,' he said.

'Since when?'

It was Bisi. She had returned with the bread and boiled egg for the guide, and so fast.

❦

Makinde earned money that month from the visitors to his lot. He was even in the Sunday newspapers.

Throngs Flock to Miracle at Mechanic's.

People came to pray for better health, success at school, new jobs, better jobs, money mostly. There were visitors in wheelchairs, blind visitors, crazy, homeless, heartbroken, childless, lonely visitors. Some people complained about the one *naira* for entrance. A few refused and walked away. One was a priest. 'How can you do this?' he asked Makinde. 'M-make money out of people's t-troubles and – and misery?'

Makinde said he could go in free (sick children and the homeless also got in free). The priest still refused to walk into his lot.

'D-did Jesus ask to be paid for miracles? How do you sleep at n-night knowing you do this for a living?'

Quite well, when he wasn't making love to Bisi, who was now talking about having a child and perhaps taking a break from her work. She became pregnant one night during a storm. Hearing the rain on his roof, Makinde worried about his Virgin Mary, though he had put a cover over the Peugeot's windscreen and put rocks on the edge of the cover to hold it in place. He was not worrying enough. During the night the wind became strong enough to move one of the rocks, and the rock dropped off the edge of the cover, which fell away from the windscreen, and the rain fell onto the windscreen and washed the vision away.

He arrived at work the next morning, and there were only two people in his lot. One was a homeless man who normally came to look for bits of food; the other was the guide woman.

'Our vision is no more,' she said.

The ground in his lot had turned to mud. Makinde could

only see the clean windscreen of the Peugeot. He was thinking about how to get back to his work.

The guide continued. 'It appears the storm last night is the cause. Our work here is done, then. We don't expect you'll have visitors any more, and as you know the Lord God gives and the . . .'

'QUIET!' Makinde shouted, so loud she ran out of his lot. The Lord God was not Makinde's favourite person at that moment. He kicked the Peugeot, which appeared to be smiling at him, and then hit it hard – so hard that his bent little finger was straightened.

He did have one visitor that day: a tax assessor.

'Mr Makinde,' he began. 'Eh, I read about you in the papers. It's been very busy here recently, eh? Since you can't call this a church, nor yourself a priest, it means that you have to pay taxes.'

Makinde had not paid taxes before. Tax was for people who wore shirts and ties, people who received cheques regularly. He thought the tax assessor was someone who had come to trick him out of his money.

'From where are you?' he asked.

'I'm from the government.'

'Couldn't they give you a clean shirt?'

'This from a man wearing rags! What have you done with your money?'

Makinde felt exhausted. Perhaps the man really was a tax assessor. If so, why didn't he go to the people who had their hands full of the country's oil money, and assess them?

'This is my lot,' he said.

'Where are your papers?' the tax assessor asked.

'What papers?'

'The papers to show that the lot belongs to you.'

Makinde trembled with anger. 'My father left me this lot,' he said. 'My father found this lot. He cleared this lot. He worked on this lot.'

'So it's yours,' the tax assessor said. 'Then you must show me proof that you've paid ground rent since the land has been yours. Don't look so cross. That's a different office's business, but I'll make sure I tell them after I've assessed the tax on your earnings, eh?'

Makinde removed his shirt. The money he had earned was hidden under his bed at home. He slept on it. He wasn't going to let this visitor from the land of rich men have it.

'What is this?' the tax assessor asked, thinking that Makinde was going to hit him.

'Here I am,' Makinde said, undoing his trousers. 'Tax my head, my arms, my broken finger. Tax my legs. See. My foot is injured; tax that. Here, tax my balls, and when you finish with them . . .' He turned his backside to the tax assessor. 'Tax my ass.'

❦

The tax assessor promised he would come back with his helpers. 'You will pay,' he said. 'Or my men will help themselves to your wife.'

A wife who wouldn't even allow Makinde to touch her. She felt sick and was eating dirt now that she was pregnant. Dirt. 'I can't help it,' she said. 'When I see it, I want to touch it. When I touch it, I want to smell it. When I smell it, I want to eat it.'

Makinde watched as she put dirt into her mouth. He tried to stop her by reminding her of disease. He could not afford to take her to a doctor. He could not go to work, because he was afraid of the taxman's helpers. They argued. In the end she packed a suitcase and said she was going to her mother in the village for a week.

Makinde decided to get advice from Rasaki, a local man known as the King of Downtown. Rasaki's work was playing pools and, for a price, arranging beatings for other people. People said he was friendly with criminals and armed robbers, he smoked and drank a lot of dangerous things, and he called out to girls in the street in Lagos, 'Baby, I've got a big one!' And they replied, 'Yeah, as big as my little finger!'

That sort of King. But he was also known as a person who helped people in trouble with government offices, the police, the tax men. He knew exactly who to bribe.

Rasaki was smoking a Bicycle cigarette as Makinde talked. His fingers were as black as his lips, and his teeth were a dirty yellow. 'My friend,' he said, 'what is wrong with your head? You don't say things like that to a tax assessor.'

Makinde said quietly, 'It's too late for that advice.'

Rasaki had just woken up. He stared at the calendar on his wall. The girl of the month, Miss February, wearing very little, smiled back at him.

'Why didn't you keep your mouth shut?' Rasaki said. 'You want to offer your wife?'

'My wife,' Makinde said. 'She smells of boiled egg most

Rasaki studied the naira notes. He shook his head and smiled.
'You got this by tricking believers?'

days. Right now she eats dirt. I love her. I would not offer my wife to the President if he wanted her.'

'I thought not. And I'm telling you, these tax men are not normal human beings. They have a lot of hate in their hearts, and they want revenge. It's how they get their jobs in the first place. I suggest – and no need to take my advice, I'm only suggesting – that you pay him the money he asked for.'

'Pay?'

'Yes, because right now he's feeling terrible. You've made him feel like a small man, and nothing you do will make him feel better. From my experience, he may probably ask you to pay enough to buy the whole lot.'

'How will I ever do that?'

'How much money do you have now?'

'It's here in my pocket.'

'Put it on my table.'

Makinde did. Rasaki studied the *naira* notes. He shook his head and smiled. 'You got this by tricking believers?'

'I didn't trick anyone,' Makinde answered. 'They just paid to get in.'

'Call it whatever you want. You were in a game of chance, and you were winning. People believed you, and you tricked them. I'm not blaming you. They were all crazy, so it's their fault. Who knows what Mary looked like? Do you?'

Makinde was getting impatient. Rasaki seemed to know a lot of things, except how to help him out of paying the tax man.

'What can you do for me?' he asked.

'My friend,' Rasaki said. 'Do you play pools?'

❧

Rasaki knew everything about pools. That was how he had survived without a job for years. Playing pools was not dangerous, he said, and only those who played pools long enough knew this. The people who lost were the ones on the outside, like believers looking for miracles in lots.

'Give me your money and I will give you back ten times as much,' he said.

'How?' Makinde asked.

'Ah-ah? Will I tell you what has taken me years and years to learn?'

'Why should I give you what has taken me a month to earn?'

'It's up to you.'

'I don't have many choices.'

'The possibilities are endless.'

'You know a lot. Why aren't you a rich man yourself?'

'I choose not to be.'

'Why?'

'Where else will I be a King?'

Makinde had to agree that he did not know one person like Rasaki, who walked around downtown like a king. He wore trousers that were long and wide; 'Keep-Lagos-clean' that fashion was called. His gray hair was cut high on top; 'Girls-follow-me' that haircut was called. His girlfriends were prostitutes, he lived in one room, and people knew that his wife had left him because he could not father children, and yet he was extremely sure of himself.

'I came to you because you're a man who knows people,'

Makinde said. 'I was hoping for something not so out of the ordinary. A name to give a bribe to perhaps? Let me think about this.'

❦

At home Makinde considered the choices. There was his lot, and there was the money that he hadn't earned from working. Free money. It seemed to him that Rasaki was right. Who left his lot with a miracle? Who departed with more money in their pockets, except him? Those who came in wheelchairs went away in wheelchairs, those who came blind went away blind. Not one of the visitors to his lot was a Mercedes owner, those big, god-like people who controlled his country. It didn't matter how long he worked, life would always suit their plans, their wishes. Never his. Never his.

He thought. He worried. He could not find an answer that pleased him. In the end he went back to Rasaki with the money. Rasaki promised a return within a week.

❦

How did Makinde hear about his money? He kept going to Rasaki's place, but Rasaki was not there. He asked about him, and people said that he had travelled up north. He waited near the row of rough houses where the King had a room. No Rasaki. The King had completely disappeared downtown.

It wasn't until Bisi returned, full of her mother's delicious vegetables and no longer wanting to eat dirt, that he heard the news from her. She had heard it from her friend in the married women's group at church, who'd heard it from her husband, who'd heard it from a friend at work. Rasaki had taken money from someone to play pools, lost the money, and the someone would probably not ask for his money back, because the someone was in big trouble with the tax men, and Rasaki knew exactly who to approach to make sure the someone ended up ruined, and the someone was Makinde.

'Is it true?' Bisi asked him.

'It seems so,' Makinde said.

'In the short time I've been away?'

'Yes.'

'How could you?'

'I had little choice.'

'Well, it makes me sick.'

'Why?' he asked (the kind of question she would ask). After all, it was not his fault. She saw the vision on the dirty windscreen. She told people, and they came, and they stopped him from doing his work, got his name mentioned in the papers, and made the tax man notice him.

'It was your vision that made this happen,' he said.

'That's not true at all,' she said, and honestly. 'It is you who went wrong when you listened to that terrible man Rasaki. That money was a blessing. You lost it as soon as you chose the wrong way to make more money from it.'

'What other way was there?'

'Why not take it to church?'

'For what?'

'To give as tithes. God gives great blessings to those who give.'

'My dear wife, when has God ever given me a blessing?'

'It is you who went wrong when you listened to that terrible
man Rasaki. That money was a blessing,' said Bisi.

Bisi had to think. Becoming a father was one blessing, but perhaps Makinde would not want to hear that. She couldn't think of another.

'I give tithes,' she said. 'My prayers are answered.'

'The miracle you prayed for on my lot, was that answered?'

'No.'

'Ah, well.'

'It will be! I know it will!'

'Tell me when that happens. Me, I feel like I've been fighting against something much stronger than me. It's ruined my life, and I don't want to fight it any more.'

She had an answer to their problem meanwhile. She could get help from the married women's group, who had money put away for emergencies. 'But you have to join my church family.'

Makinde was truly exhausted. 'For God's sake.'

'It's the rule. You want this help or not?'

'I don't think I've got any choice.'

The following Sunday he went to Abundant Life Tabernacle with Bisi. There Bisi told him that the miracle she prayed for had happened – he was present in her church. 'I'm so glad you found your way,' she said.

GLOSSARY

affair a secret sexual relationship between two people

ass *(American, taboo, slang)* the part of the body you sit on, your bottom, your backside

assess to calculate the amount or value of something

balls *(taboo, slang)* a man's testicles; also, courage, bravery

Bible the holy book of the Christian religion

blessing something that is good or helpful

bride a woman on her wedding day

bridegroom a man on his wedding day

ceremony a formal public or religious event

clerk a person whose job is to keep records in an office

community all the people who live in a particular place

conductor a person who sells or checks tickets on a bus

corset a piece of women's underwear, fitting the body tightly, (now old-fashioned)

coup a sudden, illegal, and often violent change of government

darling a word for someone that you love very much

duty something that you feel you have to do because it is right

election a time when people vote to choose a new government

estate a large area of land (not in a town), owned by one person

ethnic belonging to a race or people with their own traditions

exile having to live in a country that is not your own

evil very bad; harmful

gossip to talk about other people's private lives, often unkindly

gourd   a large fruit with a hard skin

government   the group of people who control a country

independence   the time when a country gets its freedom from control by another country

joy   a feeling of great happiness

lot *(n)*   an area of land

maize   a tall plant grown for its large yellow grains

mine *(n)*   a large hole under the ground where people dig for coal, gold, etc.; **miner** *(n)* a person who works in a mine

miracle   a wonderful and surprising event that cannot be explained by the laws of nature

missionary   a person who is sent to a foreign country to teach people about Christianity

mistress   a woman in a sexual relationship with a man who is not her husband

politics   the activities connected with using power in public life; *(adj)* **political**; *(n)* **politician**

pools   a kind of gambling in which people bet on the results of football matches

pray   to speak privately to God

pregnant   expecting a baby

priest   a person who carries out religious duties and ceremonies in a church

prostitute   a person who has sex for money

rag   a rough piece of old cloth, used for cleaning things

regime   a kind of government, especially one that has not been elected in a fair way

religious   connected with a belief in a god or gods; believing strongly in a god or gods

research *(n)*   detailed study to discover new facts or information

respect *(n)* having a high opinion of someone and behaving with
    great politeness towards them
ruin *(v)* to damage something badly; to destroy somebody's
    reputation
rule what must or should be done (in a place of work, when
    playing a game, etc.)
soothsayer a person who can see into the future, or so some
    people believe
swing *(v)* to turn or change direction suddenly
tax *(n)* money that people have to pay to the government
tithe a tenth of a person's income, that they give to the church
traditional following ideas, beliefs, and customs that have not
    changed for a long time
trick to make somebody believe something that is not true, in
    order to cheat them
Virgin Mary the mother of Jesus Christ, thought to be a very
    holy person in some religions
vision a picture in your imagination, a kind of dream, especially
    of a religious kind
windscreen the window across the front of a car
World Gospel Crusading Alliance the name of an invented
    American religious organisation that sends missionaries all
    over the world

ACTIVITIES

Before Reading

Before you read the stories, read the introductions at the beginning, then use these activities to help you think about the stories. How much can you guess or predict?

1 *The Truly Married Woman* (story introduction page 1). What do you think is the best way for a wife to get a husband to do what she wants? Choose one or more of these.

1 give him an order	4 cry a lot
2 say nice things to him	5 argue until he agrees
3 make a quiet suggestion	6 cook him a special meal

2 *The Road to Migowi* (story introduction page 15). Every job has its boring side. Think of one good and one bad thing about each of these jobs.

1 doctor	5 factory worker
2 bus driver	6 shop assistant
3 cook	7 president
4 news reporter	8 builder

3 *Two Sisters* (story introduction page 22). How should sisters behave towards one another? Discuss these ideas.

1 An older sister should look after a younger sister.
2 An older sister should give advice to a younger sister.
3 An older sister should leave a younger sister to live her own life.

4　A younger sister should make her own decisions.

5　A younger sister should listen to an older sister.

6　A younger sister should argue with an older sister if she doesn't agree with her.

4　*Blood Feuds* (story introduction page 40). **What do you think would be the worst thing about living in exile? Put these ideas in order of (a) to (f), starting with (a) for the worst thing.**

1　You are not really part of the country you live in.

2　You do not see some members of your family very often.

3　You cannot work to change your country's future.

4　When you go back, people have forgotten about you or don't accept you.

5　When you go back, your country is different from the country of your memories.

6　You feel you do not belong to either country.

5　*The Miracle Worker* (story introduction page 55). **What do you think a miracle is? Choose one or more of these meanings.**

1　some very good news

2　a lucky thing that you did not expect or think possible

3　an act that does not follow the laws of nature and is thought to be caused by God

4　a reward for good work or a good action

5　a very good example of something

6　something that you want very much

ACTIVITIES

After Reading

1 **Here are the thoughts of five characters (one from each story). Who is thinking, in which story, and what has just happened in the story?**

1 'They're laughing – that's good. I've got to keep them out of the house. I hate saying these things about him, because he's so dear to me, but I must make everybody believe that he's gone. Perhaps my daughter can help. . .'

2 'Of course I'm not ill. Silly man! He still doesn't understand, does he? Yesterday wasn't just about a dress and a cake. I can see that I'll have to tell him exactly how things are going to be in this house from now on . . .'

3 'That's life. I tried to help him – but it doesn't always work. I think it's time for a little holiday. And if he comes looking for me, and for his money – well, I know a few people I can talk to. I won't get any trouble from him.'

4 'What do they expect? Do they think I'm going back to a life with no good times, no new shoes, just a boring job and maybe a stupid husband? Oh no! She was happy to take that motor, so she can stop looking at me like that . . .'

5 'What a day! So much rain and mud. But it keeps me going, driving up and down this road. And now at last we're back on the road. Why's he looking so strange though? What's worrying him? I think I'd better just get on and drive . . .'

2 **Complete this conversation between Mwali and her husband from *Blood Feuds* on the night after the lorries are burnt. Use as many words as you like.**

MWALI: It wasn't thieves who burnt the lorries. We both know that. What are we going to do?

HUSBAND: Your father thinks that I _____.

MWALI: Perhaps he's right. Perhaps it's safer that way.

HUSBAND: Who can say? I just know that I don't want _____.

MWALI: What if you go home to your family, and I join you later, with the children?

HUSBAND: I'm sure that, with the elections coming, there _____. If that happens, you and the children may not be able to _____.

MWALI: And then we could be separated for months, or years!

HUSBAND: Perhaps we should _____. Who knows, after a while perhaps the trouble _____.

MWALI: That's true, but things can change very quickly.

HUSBAND: And of course your father can't _____. He's an old man now.

MWALI: So we're back at the beginning. Oh, what's the best thing to do? I just don't know.

HUSBAND: Listen, Mwali. We can _____, or we can _____, but I think we should all _____, whatever happens.

MWALI: You're right. Families belong together. We'll tell my father in the morning.

3 Here is a conversation between Bisi, in *The Miracle Worker*, and her friend from church about the lost money. Put their conversation in the right order and write in 'Bisi' or 'Friend' for the speakers' names. The friend speaks first (number 4).

1 _____ 'Ah! And if he asks for the money back, Rasaki will say a few words to the right person . . .'

2 _____ 'No, I've been away. What news is that?'

3 _____ 'Oh Bisi, haven't you guessed? It's Makinde!'

4 _____ 'Well, Bisi, have you heard the news?'

5 _____ 'I don't think so. You see, this someone we know is in a lot of trouble with the tax man.'

6 _____ 'This is a sad story. But tell me, who is this someone we know?'

7 _____ 'It's about Rasaki. Someone we know gave him a lot of money to play pools, and he's gone and lost it all!'

8 _____ 'Exactly. And someone we know will be in even more trouble than he is now.'

9 _____ 'That's terrible! But can't this person get the money back from Rasaki?'

4 What happens next? Read the notes below for two of the stories, and choose which ending you prefer, (a) or (b). Then write a paragraph to make a new ending, using the notes.

The Truly Married Woman

a) Ajayi surprised, then angry / leaves house / Ayo cries / wishes for things as before / Ajayi returns / things never quite the same

b) Ajayi surprised, but agrees / after baby born, Ayo fat and

happy / takes control of house / Ajayi follows orders /
sometimes sorry he married

Two Sisters

a) Mercy argues with sister / stops visiting / Connie sees her
in town from time to time / polite / talk like strangers

b) Connie refuses to meet friend / sends Mercy away / still
worries / sees photo in papers / hopes Mercy will change

5 Which story did you like best, and why?

6 Here is a short poem (a kind of poem called a haiku) about one
of the stories. Which of the five stories is it about?

> *Yes, he has a wife.*
> *It doesn't matter to me –*
> *no advice, thank you!*

Here is another haiku,
about the same story.

> *Young and beautiful*
> *she has so much still to learn –*
> *but I must not speak.*

A haiku is a Japanese poem, which is always in three lines, and
the three lines always have 5, 7, and 5 syllables each, like this:

| Yes | he | has | a | wife | = 5 syllables
| It | does | n't | mat | ter | to | me | = 7 syllables
| no | ad | vice | thank | you | = 5 syllables

Now write your own haiku, one for each of the other four
stories. Think about what each story is really about. What are
the important ideas for you? Remember to keep to three lines
of 5, 7, 5 syllables each.

ABOUT THE AUTHORS

ABIOSEH NICOL

Davidson Sylvester Hector Willoughby Nicol (1924–1994) was born in Freetown, Sierra Leone. He also had an African name, Abioseh, which means 'born on a Sunday', and he used this name for his published fiction. He was educated in Sierra Leone, Nigeria, and the UK, where he studied sciences and medicine. After some years of medical research in the UK, he became a teacher and administrator at universities in Nigeria and Sierra Leone, and was Vice-Chancellor of the University of Sierra Leone from 1966 to 1969. He then began a diplomatic career and was Under-Secretary-General of the United Nations from 1972 to 1982. Meanwhile, he wrote poetry and short stories, and several works of non-fiction. His short stories were published in *Two African Tales* (1965) and *The Truly Married Woman and Other Stories* (1965). It is said of his writing that 'his poems and stories are usually set in rural villages, where he felt the true heart and spirit of Africa survive'.

KEN LIPENGA

Ken Lipenga (1952–) was born in Chiringa, Phalombe, southern Malawi, at the foot of the famous Michesi Mountain, which local people believe is the home of the spirits of their ancestors. He was educated at schools in Malawi, and gained degrees from the University of Malawi, Leeds University in the UK, and the University of New Brunswick in Canada. After several years working as a university lecturer in English, he became a newspaper editor. However, those were politically difficult times in Malawi, and he lost this job when he criticized the government of the day. In 1993 he returned to journalism, but in 1997 he was elected Member of Parliament for Phalombe East, and since then has had a number of different positions in the Malawian government. He writes both poems and short stories, and also likes fishing, photography, and mountain climbing.

AMA ATA AIDOO

Ama Ata Aidoo (1942–) was born in Abeadzi Kyiakor in central Ghana. She graduated from the University of Ghana, and has since taught in universities in Ghana, Kenya, and the United States. She decided to be a writer at the age of fifteen, and won her first competition four years later. Her writing includes poems, plays, short stories, novels, and children's books. The story 'Two Sisters' is from her short-story collection *No Sweetness Here* (1970). She won the Nelson Mandela Prize for Poetry in 1987 for *Someone Talking to Sometime*, and in 1992 her novel *Changes* won the Commonwealth Writers Prize for Best Book for the Africa Region. 'Since I am a woman,' she says, 'it is natural that I not only write about women but with women in more central roles.' The women in her stories are often trying to challenge the rules that govern the way they live their lives. She is also interested in showing people struggling with the differences between the African and Western views of the world.

PAUL TIYAMBE ZELEZA

Paul Tiyambe Zeleza (1955–) was born in Harare, Zimbabwe, to Malawian parents. His parents returned to Malawi the following year, and Zeleza grew up and went to university there. Soon after graduation he made the decision to leave Malawi so that he could write without censorship. Since then he has worked at universities in Kenya, Jamaica, Canada, and the United States, and became Professor of African American Studies at the University of Illinois at Chicago in 2007. He has published widely on African economics and history, and also has a blog called *The Zeleza Post*, where he and others write about Africa today. His works of fiction include a novel and two collections of short stories, *Night of Darkness and Other Stories* (1976) and *The Joys of Exile: Stories* (1994). He still remembers his mother's annoyance as he slowly typed his first stories with two fingers back in the 1970s: 'Because I was always writing, my mama would say, "Can't you leave the house, and go play, or go do *something*?"'

SEFI ATTA

Sefi Atta (1964–) was born in Lagos, Nigeria. She was educated in Nigeria and the UK, and trained as an accountant. She now lives in Mississippi in the United States and is a university teacher. Her stories have won many awards, and she has also written two novels, *Swallow and Everything Good Will Come*, which won the Wole Soyinka Award for Literature in Africa in 2006. A collection of her short stories, *Lawless and Other Stories*, was published in 2008. In her stories she writes the story that she wants to tell, not the one that her audience expects. 'I don't set out to offend,' she has said, 'but a story is worth writing only if I raise inconvenient questions. That doesn't always earn me approval.'

OXFORD BOOKWORMS LIBRARY

Classics • Crime & Mystery • Factfiles • Fantasy & Horror
Human Interest • Playscripts • Thriller & Adventure
True Stories • World Stories

The OXFORD BOOKWORMS LIBRARY provides enjoyable reading in English, with a wide range of classic and modern fiction, non-fiction, and plays. It includes original and adapted texts in seven carefully graded language stages, which take learners from beginner to advanced level. An overview is given on the next pages.

All Stage 1 titles are available as audio recordings, as well as over eighty other titles from Starter to Stage 6. All Starters and many titles at Stages 1 to 4 are specially recommended for younger learners. Every Bookworm is illustrated, and Starters and Factfiles have full-colour illustrations.

The OXFORD BOOKWORMS LIBRARY also offers extensive support. Each book contains an introduction to the story, notes about the author, a glossary, and activities. Additional resources include tests and worksheets, and answers for these and for the activities in the books. There is advice on running a class library, using audio recordings, and the many ways of using Oxford Bookworms in reading programmes. Resource materials are available on the website <www.oup.com/elt/bookworms>.

The *Oxford Bookworms Collection* is a series for advanced learners. It consists of volumes of short stories by well-known authors, both classic and modern. Texts are not abridged or adapted in any way, but carefully selected to be accessible to the advanced student.

You can find details and a full list of titles in the *Oxford Bookworms Library Catalogue* and *Oxford English Language Teaching Catalogues*, and on the website <www.oup.com/elt/bookworms>.

THE OXFORD BOOKWORMS LIBRARY
GRADING AND SAMPLE EXTRACTS

STARTER • 250 HEADWORDS

present simple – present continuous – imperative –
can/cannot, must – going to (future) – simple gerunds …

Her phone is ringing – but where is it?

Sally gets out of bed and looks in her bag. No phone. She looks under the bed. No phone. Then she looks behind the door. There is her phone. Sally picks up her phone and answers it. *Sally's Phone*

STAGE I • 400 HEADWORDS

… past simple – coordination with *and, but, or* –
subordination with *before, after, when, because, so* …

I knew him in Persia. He was a famous builder and I worked with him there. For a time I was his friend, but not for long. When he came to Paris, I came after him – I wanted to watch him. He was a very clever, very dangerous man. *The Phantom of the Opera*

STAGE 2 • 700 HEADWORDS

… present perfect – *will* (future) – *(don't) have to, must not, could* –
comparison of adjectives – simple *if* clauses – past continuous –
tag questions – *ask/tell* + infinitive …

While I was writing these words in my diary, I decided what to do. I must try to escape. I shall try to get down the wall outside. The window is high above the ground, but I have to try. I shall take some of the gold with me – if I escape, perhaps it will be helpful later. *Dracula*

STAGE 3 • 1000 HEADWORDS
... should, may – present perfect continuous – *used to* – past perfect –
causative – relative clauses – indirect statements ...

Of course, it was most important that no one should see
Colin, Mary, or Dickon entering the secret garden. So Colin
gave orders to the gardeners that they must all keep away
from that part of the garden in future. *The Secret Garden*

STAGE 4 • 1400 HEADWORDS
... past perfect continuous – passive (simple forms) –
would conditional clauses – indirect questions –
relatives with *where/when* – gerunds after prepositions/phrases ...

I was glad. Now Hyde could not show his face to the world
again. If he did, every honest man in London would be proud
to report him to the police. *Dr Jekyll and Mr Hyde*

STAGE 5 • 1800 HEADWORDS
... future continuous – future perfect –
passive (modals, continuous forms) –
would have conditional clauses – modals + perfect infinitive ...

If he had spoken Estella's name, I would have hit him. I was
so angry with him, and so depressed about my future, that I
could not eat the breakfast. Instead I went straight to the old
house. *Great Expectations*

STAGE 6 • 2500 HEADWORDS
... passive (infinitives, gerunds) – advanced modal meanings –
clauses of concession, condition

When I stepped up to the piano, I was confident. It was as if I
knew that the prodigy side of me really did exist. And when
I started to play, I was so caught up in how lovely I looked
that I didn't worry how I would sound. *The Joy Luck Club*

MORE WORLD STORIES FROM BOOKWORMS